Proscenophobia

A Thriller

Bettine Manktelow

A Samuel French Acting Edition

SAMUEL
FRENCH
FOUNDED 1830

SAMUELFRENCH-LONDON.CO.UK
SAMUELFRENCH.COM

PROSCENOPHOBIA
(Stage Fright)

First performed at the Astor Theatre Arts Centre, Deal, Kent on 22nd March 2001 with the following cast:

Mildred Pearce	Gilly Litton
Justin James	Pip Piacentino
Judy Rhodes	Coralie Kavanagh
Adelaide Marchbanks	Patricia Jones
Pearl Palmer	Lynda Borley
Edward Gibb	Mike Desborough

Produced and directed by **Bettine Walters**

CHARACTERS

Adelaide (Addie) Marchbanks, attractive, ambitious, larger than life, a star in every way, self-centred and very vain, 40s

Mildred (Millie) Pearce, attractive, optimistic, over-the-top actress, 40s

Judy Rhodes, assistant stage manager, neurotic and permanently anxious, hiding her true self, 20s

Justin James, the company manager, very much a man of the theatre, extravagant in speech and gesture, affected, sophisticated, imperturbable, 50-ish

Edward (Ed) Gibb, "The Husband", an impresario and aging lothario with a heart of steel who still retains his charm, 50-ish

Pearl Palmer, a little too sweet, ostensibly everybody's friend but very false and superficial, middle-aged

The action of the play takes place in Adelaide's dressing-room in a provincial theatre

Time—the present

SYNOPSIS OF SCENES

ACT I

ACT II

Other plays by Bettine Manktelow
published by Samuel French Ltd:

Curtain Call
Curtain Up on Muder
Death Walked In
They Call It Murder

ACT I

SCENE 1

Adelaide's dressing-room in a provincial theatre. Darkness

A door is RC, *an intercom* R *of the door. Against the wall* UC *is a rack of clothes,* L *is a screen. Facing* R *and* L *walls are dressing-tables with mirrors. A chair in front of each dressing-table. A couch is* DLC

Millie, in her dressing-gown, is lying asleep on the couch

Justin enters and without being aware of Millie goes to the dressing-table R, *pulls open a drawer and feels inside but doesn't find what he is looking for. He then tries to open another drawer but it is locked*

Justin (*softly*) Oh, damn!
Millie Eh? (*She raises her head drowsily*)
Justin (*startled*) Oh Addie—I didn't know you were in.
Millie It isn't Addie, it's me. Why don't you put the light on?
Justin I didn't think about it. (*He crosses and switches on the light by the side of the door*)
Millie I was making the most of the couch before Addie gets here. She isn't keen on me snoozing while she's making up.
Justin You can't blame her, darling. Not every leading lady would be prepared to share her dressing-room with her understudy.
Millie Oh, I know all about that, but we *are* old friends.
Justin With the emphasis on the old!
Millie Aren't we catty tonight?
Justin No more than usual.
Millie (*yawning and stretching*) What time is it anyway?
Justin Just on the half hour. I was looking for a prop that Judy has mislaid— silly bitch!
Millie You will employ these woebegones. Where did you get her from anyway?
Justin An advert in *The Stage*—where else? I'm afraid she does seem to have a propensity for disaster.
Millie Ah well, we're stuck with her now. It's not much longer, after all.

Where can Addie be? She's never late. More's the pity! I might have a stab at her part if she were.

Justin You could always put some soap on the stairs, darling, make sure she literally breaks a leg.

Millie I couldn't do that to my best friend, Justin. Nothing short of murder would do.

Justin I have noticed how you two love each other.

Millie We enjoy a fight. After all, what are best friends for?

Justin I sometimes wonder.

Judy enters in a panic

Judy Oh Justin, there you are. The intercom isn't working. What are we to do?

Justin (*laconically*) Ask Monty to have a look at it. It's probably just a loose wire somewhere.

Judy It's such a nuisance, everything seems to be going wrong this week.

Millie Not just this week. But why worry? We only have one more week to go. What else can go wrong?

Judy Anything can. Don't tempt fate! There've been so many minor mishaps with this production. Look at what's happened to Addie! She must have a charmed life, what with falling down the stairs in Cambridge and that bit of scenery collapsing on her head in Brighton, *and* she nearly got run over by the scenery truck when we came here. Yet she still comes up smiling.

Justin If I didn't know Millie better I'd think it was a plot!

Millie The bloody nerve! You know I'd never do anything to hurt my friend.

Judy Oh, no, Justin, it's just bad luck. It's me! I'm a jinx! I must be. Take this week—just when I thought I'd got on top of everything the intercom packs up!

Justin (*with weary lassitude*) It doesn't matter. If it can't be fixed, we'll go back to the old-fashioned way of calling the time—in person.

Judy (*dismayed*) What you mean is I'll have to go round tapping on each dressing-room every ten minutes. Oh Justin, how have I got time for that? I should have an assistant or something.

Justin An assistant for the assistant. Even a number one tour can't afford that, darling, and it's gone the half hour already.

Judy (*disgruntled*) Yes, I know. I suppose that's what I'll have to do, but I don't think it's fair.

Judy goes off, leaving the door half open

(*Off; calling*) Half an hour, please, half an hour...

Millie Dear me, she is in a state. I'm surprised she hasn't had a nervous breakdown by now.

Justin She gets like that, not at all phlegmatic. Personally, I can do without people flapping all over the place.

Millie We can't all be like you, Justin, so laid-back you're almost asleep!

Justin (*offended*) I wouldn't say I'm like that—not at all!

Addie enters in a hurry. She is smartly dressed, having been out to lunch in London

Addie What wouldn't you say, Justin? Oh, hallo, Millie. Trust me to find the company manager in my dressing-room the one time I'm late. Sorry about that. I had a late lunch at the *Ivy* and then I missed the train.

Justin It's no problem. It's only just gone the half-hour. The intercom isn't working so don't expect a call.

Addie moves to the dressing-table R and starts divesting herself of her jewellery etc.

Addie You know how reliable I am as a rule, Justin, and I have a good excuse. I was looking for an angel.

Millie But angels are so few...

Addie You look as if you've been slumbering on my couch again, darling.

Millie It's half mine. I was only slumbering on my half! I thought you wouldn't mind.

Addie Well, I do mind. I want some peace before the show starts and time to unwind. I don't want to be faced with an invasion in my dressing-room.

Millie It is my dressing-room too. Anyway, one small person doesn't constitute an invasion in anybody's language, darling. You can't count Justin.

Justin No, you can't count me.

Addie The thing that annoys me, Justin, is that I have allowed Millie to share my dressing-room this week, because she hates sharing with Pearl. It was a concession on my part and I only agreed as long as Millie kept to her part over there (*she points* L) and gave me some peace before the show. After all, she only has a small part in Act II. She could swan around in the Green Room till then. (*She goes behind the screen to change*)

Millie Don't be so mean, Addie! No-one can sleep in the Green Room with all the cast coming and going, talking shop and being boring. How can anyone sleep through that?

Addie (*from behind the screen*) I don't know why she can't sleep at home like any other self-respecting actress.

Millie I do wish you'd stop talking about me in the third person, darling.

Addie All right then—why didn't you sleep at home?
Millie I missed the train last night—I didn't get home.
Addie You are silly! What did you do then?
Millie Oh, they put me up at the pub. Jolly decent of them I thought, but it
  wasn't very comfortable. I'm a bit old for couches.
Addie Except for casting couches!
Millie Especially those!
Justin Millie was about to brush up on your lines, Addie. Just in case you
  didn't turn up.
Addie (*coming out from behind the screen in her dressing-gown*) No chance!
  Come hell or high water I shall go on! Now then, I could do with a cup of
  tea.
Justin I'll see if Judy's put the kettle on. (*Sarcastically*) That is *if* she has
  time. (*He glances at his watch*) You have twenty minutes, poppets.

Justin exits

Millie I think I could do with something stronger than tea, personally.
Addie Trust you! I'll see what I can do! (*She finds the key to her dressing-
  table drawer in her handbag, and opens the drawer while speaking*) I
  thought I had pulled it off today, Millie, to be honest, but what did the old
  wretch say as soon as we were on our liqueurs. "I'll let you know". Yet I
  picked up the tab! (*She takes out a half full bottle of brandy*)
Millie Don't ring us! We'll ring you!
Addie Exactly! Find some glasses, darling, would you?

*Millie goes to her own dressing-table L and picks up some rather grubby
glasses and polishes them on her make-up towel*

Millie I wondered why you locked your drawer.
Addie How did you know? Did you try it?
Millie No, but I think Justin did. He woke me up. Apparently, they've mislaid
  a prop. (*She takes the glasses across to Addie*)
Addie Oh, the gun—it's here. It's not needed till Act II. Why the fuss?
Millie You know Judy—in her usual flap!
Addie How absurd! I could do without all this drama as soon as I come in.
  I think I have a migraine coming on. (*She pours them both a brandy*)
Millie Have you been eating chocolate?
Addie You know I never do, darling, but the white sauce had a distinctly
  cheesy taste which was so nice I ate it anyway. So, it's my own fault!
Millie Special treat was it—the *Ivy*? Got a new man? (*She goes back to the
  settee with her drink*)
Addie (*applying her make-up*) There are no new men at my age, dear! Only

old recycled ones! No, I really was looking for an angel. It looks as if that tired old comedy might fold at the Theatre Royal and they'd be prepared to take me—if I had the backing.

Millie With your tired old thriller?

Addie Oh, it's not that bad. Anyway, the one proviso is that I star. Apparently, I still have a name in theatrical circles.

Millie Yes, but what sort of name?

Addie You seem to forget I was a star once, in and out of the West End all the time, with financiers falling at my feet.

Millie Yes, but that was only when they were drunk! Anyway, what are you now? Just an old has-been.

Addie I'd rather be a has-been than a not-has-been.

Millie I suppose you mean me—you hag!

Pearl enters with a large bouquet

Pearl Look what I've found at the stage door!

Millie (*rising*) How sweet of you, darling! You shouldn't have bothered. (*She takes the flowers*) Oh—they're for you! (*She hands them to Addie*)

Addie Of course they're for me.

Pearl I wonder who they're from.

Addie I suppose you didn't look at the card.

Pearl As if I would!

Millie Who are they from?

Pearl An ardent admirer, I expect.

Addie Funny that's just what it says. From an ardent admirer—"Thanks for the memory!"

Millie My God, darling, it will take you years to work that one out! Think of all the memories you have to dredge up!

Addie Not one worth bothering with! Still, it is nice to think somebody cares. (*To Millie*) Put them in water for me, there's a sweetie!

Millie I might be your understudy but I'm not your slave.

Pearl I'll do it.

Millie You creep. I'll do it.

Millie exits with the flowers

Pearl At least she seems to be sober tonight.

Addie She is a bit naughty, I know. (*She goes back to the dressing-table* R *to continue with her make-up*) But she's bored, you see. She only has that little scene at the end of Act II and nothing to do all evening but sit around getting drunk. You can't blame her.

Pearl *You* can't blame her, everyone else can.

Addie She was awfully good once upon a time.

Pearl Weren't we all? No news about us getting into the West End, I suppose?

Addie There could be. I'm working on it.

Pearl Oh, you darling! If only we could. (*Hopefully*) You would take us, I suppose, the original cast?

Addie Of course I would. That would be part of the deal. I'd even take Millie.

Pearl You have been a good friend to her. I was only saying so the other day to Judy, what a good friend Addie has been to that awful Millie!

Addie Oh, shush! She isn't that bad, and I like to do a good turn for people. I'm like that! Besides, it's such a small cast, we have to try to get along together.

Pearl I could never get along with her any more after the way she treated my Guy.

Addie Your guy? I didn't know you had one. What happened?

Pearl My son Guy, I mean. When he came to see the show and we had drinks afterwards, she practically ate him alive! All the way back on the train she was trying to seduce him.

Addie Oh, surely not on the train! It's so public.

Pearl I don't mean literally, but making it obvious she would if he would. She terrified him! After all, he's half her age—well, almost.

Addie As I said she is naughty but she means well! (*She goes behind the screen to change*)

Pearl I hate to think what she means!

Millie enters with the flowers in a vase

Millie Here they are—don't they look pretty? Oh, you still here?

Pearl I'm just going to put my face on.

Millie Yes, you need to.

Pearl Just what do you mean by that?

Millie At our age, darling, we all need a little skilful aid from the beauty box.

Pearl I'm talking about my stage make-up.

Millie So am I! But you must be more careful, darling, your mascara was so smudged last night I thought you had two black eyes. You really should use a magnifying mirror.

Pearl (*indignantly*) Don't you try to tell me how to make up. I was in the theatre when——

Millie When what? When Addie and I were in kindergarten, I suppose!

Pearl Certainly not!

Millie You nearly gave yourself away then, didn't you? You'll have to tell me some day what it was like to work with Ellen Terry.

Pearl Oh, Addie—this woman is incorrigible!

Pearl slams out

Addie (*laughing from behind the screen*) Millie, you are very naughty sometimes!

Millie Oh, she just gets on my wick, that one. She's a real old theatrical snob, name-dropping all over the place. Talking about the old days when she was something, when she never was anything anyway. Who's heard of her now?

Addie Who's heard of any of us now? Fame is transitory. Anyway, you offended her, making a play for her son.

Millie What do you mean?

Addie Her son Guy. She said you tried to seduce him on the train.

Millie What balderdash! We exchanged pleasantries—no more!

Addie I know about your pleasantries, darling! I've seen you in action before! So I have some sympathy for poor Pearl! (*She comes out from behind the screen and goes over for Millie to button up the back of her dress*)

Millie (*helping her with her dress*) To what are you alluding?

Addie Don't play the innocent with me, you know very well!

Millie I suppose I do, but you forgave me years ago.

Addie I forgave both of you. I'm like that. Magnanimous to the core!

Judy enters with two mugs of tea on a tray

Judy Justin said you wanted some tea. It's gone the half hour. The speakers aren't working.

Addie Thank you for telling us. But I'm professional enough to keep an eye on the time myself.

Judy (*putting the tray down on Addie's dressing-table*) Oh, I see you have the flowers. Do you know who they're from?

Addie Of course. A secret admirer.

Millie If I find out who he is I'll go and kick his guide dog. (*She goes to sit on the couch*)

Addie Take no notice of her, Judy. She's only jealous.

Judy I thought it might have been your regular, that man who's been in the front row ogling you, at least three times this week.

Addie Who could that be?

Millie You know damn well! I've seen you wandering down stage when he's sitting there. Overdoing it as usual.

Addie Overdoing nothing. I was feeling the part.

Millie Yes—but whose part? A few more steps and you would have been in his lap!

Addie (*in a Mae West pose, one hand on her hip, the other behind her head*)

I have this powerful sexual magnetism. I always have. It's nothing to do with looks.

Millie Just as well!

Judy (*taking them their tea*) The way you two go on—anybody would think you didn't like each other.

Millie ⎫ (*together*) We don't!
Addie ⎭

Judy That article in *Show Talk* said you'd known one another for years.

Addie Oh God, did you read that? They put that out before the tour and it was mostly lies!

Millie We were never interviewed for it, you know.

Judy You mean it was all made up.

Addie goes to sit next to Millie on the settee, moving her across with a gentle kick on her ankle

Addie Not exactly made up.

Millie Just dug up!

Judy Still, Justin says there's no such thing as bad publicity.

Addie That depends. Nobody wants a spotlight on the far distant past—not even actresses!

Millie Particularly actresses! (*She laughs*) My dear old friend is very conscious of her age, you see, Judy. Having knocked ten years off yonks ago, she doesn't like people prying too hard into her past.

Addie (*uncomfortably*) A lady is entitled to lie about her age. It's just awkward getting caught.

Judy But you haven't. It didn't mention your age—either of you. It just said that you'd known each other for years, and you were re-united in this play.

Millie And we were both once married to the same man.

Judy Yes, they mentioned that. I must say it does seem—weird!

Addie What's weird about it? We were such good friends we decided to share everything.

Judy Who had him first?

Addie ⎫ (*together*) ⎱ I did.
Millie ⎭   ⎰ She did.

Judy What happened? Or don't you want me to know?

Addie I couldn't care less who knows.

Millie I pinched him.

Judy Golly! And you're still friends?

Addie We weren't for a while, until he dumped her for a younger model. Then I felt sorry for her.

Millie We were friends before, you see, before Addie met Ed. We were in Rep together—years ago.

Addie A few years ago.

Millie In fact when Addie married Ed I felt jealous of losing her friendship—not of him.

Addie Did you? How sweet! I had no idea.

Judy Were you married to him for long?

Addie Five years.

Judy And you?

Millie Only two.

Judy It's strange that you're still friends. I knew a woman once who was so jealous of her husband's ex-wife she plotted to kill her, even though the man they'd both been married to was dead by then.

Millie The female of the species is deadlier than the male, everyone knows that!

Justin enters

Justin Judy, I've been looking for you everywhere. Monty wants to test the intercom before the curtain goes up and you stand here chatting!

Judy (*hurt*) I only came to bring them a cup of tea, Justin.

Justin Fair enough, but don't dawdle about it! Half the props aren't set yet!

Judy (*with a hurt glance at him*) Sorry but I can't be everywhere at once!

Judy goes off; even her back looks offended

Justin That girl, when she isn't flapping she's sulking. She won't speak to me for half an hour now!

Millie That's a bonus!

Addie There's something about her I like though. Reminds me of myself when young; keen, ingenuous, trusting.

Millie God Almighty! When were you ever ingenuous or trusting! That must have been in another life.

Addie I was young once, darling. Don't forget, we were all born virgins, dear—even you!

Justin (*talking to them over the back of the settee*) You two should be in *Cats*. You wouldn't have to act.

Millie She doesn't anyway.

Addie I could out-act you any day of the week—or night.

Millie Ah, yes—Ed told me, you were very good at acting between the sheets.

Addie What do you mean by that? I never faked anything. I didn't have to.

Millie No, but he did!

Addie I don't believe it! You bitch!

Justin I'd just better leave you two to scratch each other's eyes out. I have to get this show on the road.

Addie (*rising to stop him leaving*) Oh—darling, before you go, I'm expecting a guest—quite an important one. I daresay he'll want to come backstage.

Justin I'll show him round. What's his name?

Addie Edward Gibb. He's an angel.

Justin Well, if anyone can clip his wings, you can.

Millie (*delighted*) Ed—our husband is coming to see us?

Addie Don't get too excited, darling. He isn't coming to see us. He's coming to see *me*.

Justin So we're still looking for a backer? Lunch at the *Ivy* didn't deliver one?

Addie I planted the seeds of interest.

Millie But will they grow?

Justin We might all be looking for a job next month, then.

Addie I'll let you know as soon as I know something, darling, I promise.

Justin I should hope so. (*Severely*) I invested in this tour quite heavily, Addie, as you know. We've spent twenty weeks trotting around the provinces, as near to London as we can get without actually being there. We've played to indifferent business and we still haven't a backer to take us into town or a theatre to play in. Somebody has slipped up somewhere.

Addie I'm sure I've done my best. We need more publicity.

Justin I don't think all the publicity in the world could save us now.

Addie I don't know what more I can do. There must be a way to keep going. After all, *The Mousetrap* nearly folded after a few months, and then miraculously took off. Nobody knows why.

Justin We all wish we did! Ah well, I suppose we have to accept the inevitable. The dole queue beckons!

Justin exits, looking aggrieved

Addie Poor Justin, he did sink money into this tour.

Millie So did you.

Addie Don't remind me. I re-mortgaged my house.

Millie I thought your last one left you quite well off.

Addie Of course he didn't, darling. He left me with a heap of debts after running away with an usherette. Ed is the last resort.

Millie You're not asking our husband for money.

Addie Why not? He might enjoy investing in a good little thriller like this.

Millie A minute ago it was a tired old thriller.

Addie I never said that.

Millie You did! Anyway I'm surprised you had the nerve to ask our ex for finance. What a cheek!

Addie I haven't actually asked him yet.

Millie You haven't?

Addie No, but I will tonight. Why not? He must be loaded. He has to be. He owes it to me.

Millie He owes it to both of us. But as I remember his last play folded.

Addie Oh, he must have been insured against that. And he's always made good investments apart from the theatre. He must have some spare cash.

Millie So you think he'll be your angel?

Addie One of them. The others would follow. Edward Gibb is still well known. He used to put on some marvellous shows in the old days.

Millie The problem is it *was* the old days. Nothing so transitory as fame, darling, as you're always saying.

Addie I expect he's as keen as I am on making a comeback.

Millie Let's see—which wife is he on now? Do we know? Is it number four or number five?

Addie I've lost count, and I really don't care. I was the first. I had the best.

Millie I was the second. I had the rest.

They both laugh

Thank God we didn't have kids.

Addie Yes, strange that with all his wives he's never had kids.

Millie He never wanted any.

Addie Too selfish!

Millie Like us!

Addie (*thoughtfully*) I suppose so.

Millie I'm not all that keen on seeing him, actually. I've changed.

Addie Yes, darling, you have bags under your bags. Haggard, I think, the look is! It was the in thing in the Seventies but looks a bit passé now.

Millie I can't help it if I drowned my sorrows in drink after he left me, the blighter.

Addie A pity you let yourself go. You might have got yourself another husband after Ed left, like I did.

Millie I didn't want another husband after Ed left.

Addie Hard act to follow?

Millie (*with a wry smile*) Oh, I wouldn't say that, dear. Not all the time.

Addie Ah well, he was slowing down a bit when you got him. He was all right in my days.

Millie So he was prepared to come along at a moment's notice to the sticks just to see little old you! No previous engagements? That's odd!

Addie He seemed quite keen.

Millie That's even odder!

Addie You're such a cynic.

Millie And he didn't ask for another seat? No dolly bird on his arm!

Addie Apparently not. I offered him two.

Millie The times they are a-changing!

Addie Perhaps the old dear's past it at last!

Millie Aren't we all?

Addie You speak for yourself.

Millie I am.

Addie I don't care about the personal bit, but I still care about the theatre. I want to make a comeback so badly. But—you know that. I was always much more ambitious than you.

Millie As far as I'm concerned it's just been a living. It's too late for me to get anywhere, now. You should just face it, it's too late for you. Who's heard of you these days? Only a few old has-beens like yourself.

Addie You're just jealous. You hate to think I might make a comeback.

Millie I'd love it, as long as I tag along as your understudy. But what you seem to forget, darling, is I know all about you. I knew you when...

Addie When what?

Millie When you were plain Annie March, not glamorous Addie Marchbanks. What a made-up name!

Addie No worse than some tatty old Joan Crawford character like Mildred Pearce!

Millie At least she won an Oscar!

Addie That's more than you'll ever do!

Millie I'm not alone there!

Addie All right! Maybe we are a couple of old has-beens but I'm not prepared to give up yet.

Millie No, you're right. It's worth a try. Perhaps old Ed will turn up trumps and help us out. That'll be an even bigger scoop for the gossip columns. Impresario backs play starring two ex-wives!

Addie (*sourly*) We wouldn't both be starring, duckie, don't forget that! Oh, my head, it doesn't get any better. It's positively throbbing, it must have been the cheese!

Millie Why don't you rest, dear? It will do you good.

Addie What—and let you take over when Ed's here—I just couldn't.

Millie (*crossing to her dressing-table* L) I know the part.

Addie You say you know it! But it's hardly fair to give the audience less than the best, is it?

Millie Bitch!

There is a knock at the door

Come in!

Ed enters

Ed Hi, darling! (*He goes up to Addie*)

Addie Darling!

Ed and Addie embrace

Ed (*seeing Millie*) Oh, Millie, too. I heard that you were here!
Millie Lovely to see you, Ed, after all this time! (*She crosses to him* C)

Ed and Millie embrace

Ed Delighted to see you, too, darling, just like old times. The three of us
  together. So, you're understudying Addie. I don't know how you can do it.
Millie Strictly for the money!
Ed Addie's lucky! A provincial tour doesn't usually merit understudies.
Addie I demanded it. My agent demanded it. My health demanded it. In fact,
  I've got a migraine right now.
Millie (*steering him on to the settee*) Never mind that—it's lovely to see you,
  darling. You're looking so well.
Ed I feel well. Retirement agrees with me.
Millie Have you retired? You lucky thing!
Ed Oh—sort of. I still dabble, but not like the old days.
Millie Those musicals you used to push out on the road—those were the
  days.
Addie All those leggy chorus girls!
Ed Perks of the job.
Millie Funny you settled for us.
Ed We all have our idiosyncrasies.
Addie We all make mistakes.

They all laugh

Millie Who is your latest, darling? You're surely not a bachelor again.
Ed 'Fraid so, the last one left me, cleaned me out first.
Addie Just like my last one! What a bitch!
Ed (*aghast*) Not a woman!
Addie No, I mean life's a bitch...
Millie And then you die!

They laugh

Ed Not yet though. I've got some living to do yet.
Addie I thought you'd lived at least three lives, darling!
Ed No, I just look as though I have!
Millie Oh, you've worn quite well, really. We all have, don't you think? And
  without plastic surgery!

Ed You speak for yourself!

They laugh

So what's this play about? I didn't read the reviews.

Addie There weren't any. It's just a run-of-the-mill thriller, but it has one very good acting part—mine!

Ed I might have known it! And you would like my opinion as to whether it would transfer, is that it?

Millie Oh—more than your opinion, darling!

Addie (*quickly*) All in good time—sweetie! My head's throbbing fit to burst. Won't you be a dear, Millie, and find out if there are any aspirins around back stage? I'm really suffering.

Millie I'm not your messenger girl. Go yourself. I have to get changed.

Addie Bitch! (*She goes up to the door, calling*) Judy, Judy...! (*To the others*) Won't be a mo...

Addie exits

Ed Are you in this thing as well?

Millie Small part in Act II, but if you blink you'll miss me. If I have to go on for Addie, the prop girl plays my part, only that's never happened yet. She must be as sick of it as I am.

Ed Still, it keeps the wolf from the door.

Millie Oh, I've never worried about keeping the wolf from the door, darling, just as long as he comes inside! (*She laughs*)

Ed (*fondly*) Same old Millie!

Millie Same old Ed!

Ed I must say you're looking very well, darling. I remember now why I fancied you.

Millie Don't try your fatal charm on me, sweetie, it might work!

Ed I wouldn't mind.

Millie Yes, you would. You've forgotten what I'm really like. Anyway, listen, don't waste time flirting. Do you know why she really wanted you to be here tonight?

Ed Why—she's still fond of me, wanted my opinion and all that.

Millie Much more than your opinion, sweetie... She wants your pocket book.

Ed What do you mean?

Millie She wants you to invest so we can get it to the West End.

Ed Me to invest! That's a joke!

Millie Why?

Ed (*disconsolately*) I'm broke!

Millie I don't believe it!

Ed (*rising and pacing*) I am, too many wives and too few investments, and those I had were no good. The investments I mean, not the wives! No, I was hoping that Addie would invest in something for me, actually.

Millie Oo—what?

Ed (*modestly*) Something of my own, actually.

Millie Something of your own?

Ed (*going behind the settee and sitting on the arm* L) I've written a play.

Millie Good God! After all this time presenting them you actually write something!

Ed Yes, I feel a bit embarrassed about it, actually, but it really is all my own work. There are two very good acting parts—in fact I had you both in mind when I wrote it.

Millie That's very flattering!

Ed No, I mean it.

Millie So—why can't you invest in it yourself?

Ed Because as I said, darling, I'm broke!

Millie Oh, that's great! That's good! She's hoping you'll invest and you're hoping she'll invest. And you're both broke.

Ed She's broke too!

Millie We all are. Isn't it sickening?

Ed Oh, damn! (*He rises*) What a waste of an evening!

Millie And the flowers! I presume they were from you.

Ed Oh, hell, I'd forgotten the flowers. Another twenty quid down the drain.

Millie Only twenty quid—tut, tut!

Ed How am I going to get through the evening now? I don't really want to see the wretched play.

Millie You'll just have to pretend. You can do that. I always said you should have been an actor, not an impresario.

Ed But I was once, you've forgotten. That's how I met Addie. We played a passionate love scene and didn't know when to stop. (*He sits next to her on the settee*)

Millie That, my dear, was always your trouble.

Ed Not any more. I'm older and wiser now.

Millie Being older doesn't necessarily make you wiser. It hasn't affected me!

Ed Attractive women don't have to be wise!

Millie Stop flirting!

Ed I can't break the habit of a lifetime.

Judy enters in a panic

Judy Addie has collapsed backstage. You'll have to go on, Millie!

Millie (*rising quickly*) What? My big chance and I'm not even dressed! (*She crosses to the mirror to touch up her make-up*)

Ed Is she all right? What's happened to her?

Judy I don't know! They're trying to get a doctor. But the curtain goes up in five minutes and we can't expect a miraculous recovery. Justin thought he might have to go in front of the tabs and tell them Miss Marchbanks is ill and would they like their money back.

Millie What cheek! Of course they won't want their money back. They can see me instead.

Judy And I'll have to play your part, Millie, and I can't remember a line! Oh God, I feel so nervous I could be sick!

Ed Please don't be! One invalid is enough. (*To Millie's reflection in the mirror*) I do hope Addie's all right. I think I should go and see her.

Millie No, don't. You'll miss the beginning of the play and it's quite a complicated plot.

Ed The number of plays I've seen I can guess the plot. Where is Addie?

Millie (*shrieking at him*) Ed, you were speaking to my reflection! You know that's bad luck!

Ed Sorry, didn't think. (*To Judy*) Where is Addie?

Judy In the prop room. Come with me... (*She moves to exit*)

Millie I shall probably forget every bloody line now. How could you speak to my reflection, Ed, you should know better!

Ed Don't be tiresome, Millie, such a silly superstition. (*To Judy*) Where did you say Addie was?

Judy In the prop room. I'm sorry, I can't wait. I've got to brush up on my lines. I daren't dry up. When I'm on the stage there's no-one to prompt.

Judy exits

Millie (*looking for her script*) Oh God, I can't remember how it starts! How does the bloody thing start!

Ed "Now is the winter of our discontent..."

Millie Oh, you—go, go, go! (*She pushes him out of the door*) "Out, out, damned spot".

Ed OK, I'll go. Good luck, darling! Break a leg!

Ed exits

Millie (*realizing she has quoted from "Macbeth", leaning against the door, groaning*) Oh God, what have I said? What have I said?

CURTAIN

SCENE 2

The same. An hour and a half later

The dressing-room is darkened

Addie is lying on the couch

There is a knock on the door

Addie Come in.

Justin enters

Justin It's almost the end of Act II. I thought I'd just see how you were.
Addie (*sitting up*) Oh, I'm a lot better. Switch the light on.

Justin does so

It's the only thing that works, just lying down in the dark for half an hour
and I'm as right as ninepence!
Justin (*moving down to R of the settee*) Odd, isn't it? All the way through the
run you've been fine and nearly at the end you have one of these attacks...
Addie I hope you don't think I was swinging the lead!
Justin Of course not. Why should you? I just wondered if Millie was getting
so desperate to go on that she slipped something in your tea.
Addie Darling, you've seen too many thrillers!
Justin Just a thought. (*He wanders behind the settee, talking to her over the
back of it*) After all, knowing someone suffers from migraine, it wouldn't
be too difficult to introduce something into their diet. I mean, she must
know what you're allergic to.
Addie Cheese and chocolate mostly, but no, darling, I don't think it was a
plot. It was simply the cheesy sauce I had at lunchtime. It was my fault. I
was suspicious, so I shouldn't have eaten it. Never mind, I feel much better
now, and at least it gave Millie a chance to shine. How is she by the way?
Justin Not bad—not as good as you, but then you've had more experience.

Sound of applause from the auditorium

Addie Not much more. I've just been lucky.
Justin She must be jealous of you, though. Perhaps that's why you spar so
much.
Addie No, we've always been like that. It's a sign of friendship. You must
know that!

Millie enters at speed

Millie My God—that was awful! I never thought I'd get through it. Addie, how do you work with that idiot—Pearl—she upstaged me all the time. I was literally forced to turn my back on the audience four times—quite ruining my best scene! They couldn't see my face! (*She goes behind the screen to change her clothes*)
Addie What's wrong with that?
Millie Eh?
Addie Not seeing your face.
Millie It's no laughing matter.
Addie You can say that again.
Justin Yes, I saw her do that—Millie. Very naughty, I thought, and quite deliberate.
Millie Thank you, Justin. You should have a word with her.
Justin I will if you think it will do any good.

There is a tap on the door and Ed enters

Ed Just checking up on the invalid. How are you, darling? (*He moves to R of the settee and kisses Addie on the cheek*)
Addie Much better, thank you.
Ed You're looking better. You're looking marvellous, in fact.
Addie Thank you, darling. (*She reaches up and kisses him*)
Justin (*irritated by their endearments*) Are you enjoying it—the play, I mean?
Ed Not bad! (*Rather patronisingly*) Can't say I care for the play but you've put it together quite well.
Justin (*waspishly*) I didn't choose the play.
Ed I sometimes wonder who does.
Addie Don't be naïve, darling. I chose the play because it has a good part in it for me. That's my criteria. It doesn't have to be great art!
Ed Just as well!
Millie (*popping her head round the screen*) What about me?
Ed Oh, I thought you were wonderful, darling.
Millie (*mollified*) Thank you, darling, but what about that last scene? That woman really upset me. She quite ruined my best lines. (*She comes out from behind the screen in an evening dress*) I had to play my best scene facing upstage—or else look a complete idiot turning my back on the person I'm supposed to be talking to! She wouldn't do that to you.
Addie She daren't. She knows damn well the next night I'd retaliate.
Millie (*miserably*) For me there is no next night. (*She goes to her dressing-table*)

Justin I do feel Millie has every right to be upset, Addie. I would be in her place.

Millie Thank you, Justin.

Justin (*to Ed*) So you don't like the play?

Ed Oh no, silly play, the direction leaves much to be desired and as for the acting—except for Millie of course—still I am enjoying it. Naturally.

Justin How generous of you! I'm happy to say I'm not responsible for the direction or the choice of play. I'm just the company manager.

Ed Oh, all that bit was fine. I mean it's a good all-round production, of course it is!

Addie Such a pity I felt so ill. I feel much better now. I think I could go on.

Justin That wouldn't make much sense, though, would it, darling? Millie becoming a different person in the last act, so to speak.

Addie Do you think they'd notice? They're all dead from the neck up in the suburbs.

Millie Whether they'd notice or not you're not doing it. My big scene is coming up where I get done in. I've always wanted a death scene on stage. Haven't done one since Cleopatra.

Ed When did you ever do Shakespeare?

Millie At school.

Addie I'm surprised you can remember that far back.

Millie Darling, I can even remember when I met you!

Pearl enters

Pearl Oh Addie, darling, are you feeling better? I was so surprised when Millie stepped on the stage—quite threw me.

Millie Not far enough.

Addie Yes, darling. I'm much better. In fact I feel I could go on.

Pearl Oh—I wish you would!

Millie Well, she isn't going to. (*She rises and faces Pearl*) And you owe me an apology.

Pearl I do?

They confront one another DL

Millie Certainly. You upstaged me throughout our scene together, forcing me to turn my back on the audience four times!

Pearl Oh, I am sorry. I didn't notice.

Millie Of course you noticed. Do you think we're all wet behind the ears? You know damned well when you're upstaging someone. I'm just warning you—do it once more and you'll be sorry!

Pearl Quite the prima donna, aren't we? You seem to forget you're only an understudy!

Millie (*exasperated*) Get out before I throw you out!
Pearl It isn't your dressing-room.
Millie (*threateningly*) Did you hear me?
Pearl All right, all right, I'm going. (*In a huff*) A second-rater telling me what to do! The cheek of it!

Millie aims her hair brush

Pearl exits quickly

Millie (*putting down her hair brush*) I just can't work with that cow! If it were up to me she'd get the sack.
Justin But it isn't up to you, darling. It's up to me. I suppose I'd better go and soothe her ruffled feathers. (*With a deep sigh—then pausing as he moves to the door*) Oh—Millie, you need the gun for this scene, don't forget.
Millie It's all right, Addie has it.

Justin exits

Addie Yes, I have it. (*She goes over to her dressing-table and takes the gun out of her drawer. She then crosses and gives it to Millie*) Don't forget it, darling! You'd look a bit silly threatening your husband with your fingers!
Millie Thanks. (*She slips it in her handbag*)
Addie Poor old Pearl! You didn't have to be so beastly to her! (*She returns to sit on the settee*)
Millie Yes, I did. I did have to be. All right, I'm unwinding a bit now. But I could do with another drink.
Addie That isn't a good idea, darling, you'll forget your lines.
Millie Of course I won't. (*She moves to Addie's dressing-table and helps herself to the brandy*) I act much better when I've had a drink.
Ed No, you just think you do.
Millie Anyway, I'm going to. (*She takes the drink back to her own dressing-table*) Did you really enjoy it, Ed?
Ed I enjoyed your performance. You haven't lost the old sparkle, but as for the play—you know what I'm like. I'm very critical.
Addie You're justified, darling. It is a load of old codswallop, but the provinces love thrillers, you see.
Ed I know—that's why I've written one.
Addie You've written a play? Well, darling, how exciting. What's it about?
Ed That would be telling, but it's a good plot.
Millie I suppose all writers are trying to write another *Mousetrap*.
Ed Oh no, I hope to do better than that. (*He joins Addie on the settee*) I think

I've written a really good one, keep them all guessing till the curtain falls. In fact that's my title. *The Curtain Falls.*

Addie It must be about the theatre?

Ed It's set in a theatre. It's what I know best. I just can't write things in a domestic setting, I don't know why.

Millie Could be because you have so little experience!

Addie Or so much!

Mille and Addie laugh

Millie And are there some good acting parts?

Ed There are! Really good over-the-top parts!

Addie Oh, do tell! Anything for little me!

Ed We'll see.

Millie Don't tell her any more.

Addie What do you mean? Don't tell me any more? That sounds suspiciously like you already knew about it.

Millie I didn't say that—I mean I've got to go on and I don't want to miss anything.

Ed I promise I won't say another word. We can discuss it over drinks after the show.

Addie We could discuss it right now. I don't have to go on, and I'm sure you don't want to see the rest of this.

Millie ⎫ *(together)* ⎧ He does!
Ed ⎭ ⎩ I do!

Millie We'll discuss it after the show, all three of us—promise, Ed!

Ed Solemn promise! Scout's honour!

The front of house bell sounds—softly

Millie Oh God, I thought I heard the bell. You'd better get out front, darling. Wish me luck!

Ed You know I do.

Ed exchanges kisses with both women

Here goes—see you later.

Ed exits

Addie Dear old Ed! Do you think he's really written a play for us?

Millie Maybe just for one of us! (*She stands to check her appearance in the mirror*)

Addie One of us?

Millie Why are you worried? You've got a finger in so many pies. You don't need one more.

Addie You know that isn't true. Besides, I like working with Ed.

Millie You're not going to tell me you're still a little bit in love with him?

Addie Of course not. I just admire his talent, that's all!

Millie Talent for what? Nobody knows if he's any good as a writer. He's never written anything before. For all we know he might have stolen it—you know like that play we did where the playwright steals a script from a friend and has to murder him to shut him up.

Addie Ed would never murder anyone.

Millie He might bribe someone, though.

Addie I don't think so. What's got into you?

Millie Oh—I don't trust anyone these days, sharks and sheep—everyone seems to be one or the other. A predator or a victim.

Addie Which are you?

Millie I haven't decided yet.

Judy rushes in. She is wearing different clothes—for her part in Act II

Judy Millie, you have got the gun, haven't you?

Millie What?

Judy The gun! You need it in this act. Tell me you have got it!

Millie I have—don't panic! (*She takes it out of her handbag*)

Judy Oh, thank God for that!

Addie (*reproving*) You shouldn't flap, dear. You have to keep your cool backstage.

Judy I know, but something like this is important. It is my responsibility. I shouldn't let it out of my sight except when it's on stage. The police explained it all to me. Even a replica gun could be stolen and used in a robbery. And this isn't a replica. It's the genuine article—only with blanks.

Millie I'm terrified of guns. (*She turns it over in her hands*)

Addie There's no need to be. It can't fire itself. You should worry more about the person who's using it.

Millie Yes—and that's me!

Addie I see what you mean...

Judy What a relief that's sorted out. (*To Millie*) What do you think of my outfit? Do I look like you?

Millie No comment!

Addie Yes, dear—very nice!

Judy (*glaring at Millie*) You've got about one minute, by the way.

Judy exits

Millie (*mimicking her*) One minute by the way! Do I look like you? What a cheek! (*She picks her script up from the dressing-table, thumbs through it*) Now, where am I? I've seen you play this scene often enough, Addie, but I want to do it a bit differently. Not quite so hysterical.

Addie Suit yourself.

Millie Restrained passion. (*She move to* DS) "My God—no, no you're not leaving me! I can't bear it! I can't bear it!" (*She puts the gun to her head*) Then turn the gun on myself and bang—drop down dead! Quite a good twist that, because she only intends to frighten him by firing a blank and someone has substituted the real thing which kills her and yet in fact she kills herself! I like that!

Addie Yes, it's not a bad little thriller. Ed is just too critical.

Millie He admits it, though, doesn't he? (*She puts the gun back in her handbag*) I wish I didn't have to die in this scene. I'll miss out on the ending of the play and I'm just beginning to enjoy it. I'll make the most of my death scene.

Music off stage

Addie I'm sure you will.

Millie God—I can hear the opening music. Here I go!

Millie exits

Addie goes over to her dressing-table and begins to tidy her face and hair in the mirror

After a moment Ed enters

Addie (*looking round, surprised*) The curtain's going up. What are you doing here?

Ed I think I'll miss the rest. It is rather boring.

Addie You're such an egotist. You really only enjoy your own productions.

Ed Don't we all? Are you feeling better now? I was really quite concerned.

Addie Yes, I'm much better. Would you like a drink?

Ed Is there any left?

Addie After Millie's been at it, you mean? (*She pours them both a drink*) She only started drinking after you left, you know.

Ed Now, don't make me feel guilty!

Addie As if I would! Here's to us!

Ed All of us! (*They sit on the settee to enjoy their drinks*) So now you can tell me why you asked me here. Cut the flannel about longing to see me and so on. What was the real reason?

Addie You know I love to see you…
Ed The real reason.
Addie You mean Millie hasn't told you? She never could keep anything to herself.
Ed We-ell.
Addie Exactly—she's told you all right.
Ed Darling, you know I'd love to help you out, but I'm broke. As a matter of fact I was hoping you'd invest in my play.
Addie Not a chance!
Ed (*gloomily*) We're both in the same boat, it seems.
Addie As ever. Still, you can tell me about it. What's it about?
Ed Two middle-aged actresses who hate one another but can't seem to keep away from each other.
Addie I wonder who they can be! So where does the thrilling bit come in?
Ed One gets murdered and the suspicion falls on the other one.
Addie Naturally! And is there a twist?
Ed Yes. (*He smiles*) You did it all the time.
Addie And do you see us both in it? Millie and me?
Ed I'm thinking about it.
Addie (*going back to the dressing-table to replenish her drink*) I still have a name, you know. I'm not desperate for work. (*Vaguely*) I have had offers. I would have liked this play to transfer though. I've made quite an investment in it.
Ed Sorry I can't help you out. But what am I to do now? I thought it would be quite a coup getting you two together again. Good publicity angle!
Addie We're together now.
Ed No—you're not. Millie is just an understudy. You've made her do her penance. Now you must forgive her.
Addie What, for stealing you?
Ed (*rising to face her*) She didn't so much steal me as you threw me away.
Addie Of course I didn't!
Ed You did! You always put your career first.
Addie Before what?
Ed Before *my* career!
Addie Why shouldn't I? Anyway, I forgave you both—long ago!
Ed Are you sure?
Addie Of course I am.

A shot rings out

Ed What was that?
Addie (*casually*) Oh—Millie's shot herself.
Ed What?

Addie In the play. I do hope she didn't make a hash of it. She said she's terrified of guns. It's no good if you intend to kill yourself holding the gun out here somewhere and closing your eyes. You might miss and then where would you be?

Ed Alive—presumably.

Screaming and pandemonium break out backstage

My God, that sounds realistic. Who is it?

Addie Whoever it is, it isn't in the script. (*She goes to the door*)

The door opens and Judy rushes in

Judy She's done it—she's done it—she's really done it!

Addie Who's done what?

Judy Millie—she's shot herself! She's really shot herself! (*She pauses, she looks from one to the other of them in horror*) I think she's dead!

CURTAIN

ACT II

The dressing-room. Two days later

Justin is standing on a small step ladder adjusting the intercom speaker R of the door

Judy enters

Judy (*catching sight of Justin*) I was looking for you. What do you want me to do next? All the props are packed and they're coming to collect the furniture tomorrow.

Justin Oh, the costumes, dear. I've just about finished here, but there's a load of things to go back to Nathan's.

Judy Then I'll get on with it. (*She pulls back the screen L and begins to take things off the clothes rail and put them on the settee, prior to packing*) Horrid way to end a run, isn't it? Everybody's so depressed.

Justin Closing a play is always a dismal business, but particularly under these circumstances.

Judy goes behind the screen to bring out a large box or boxes in which to pack the clothes

Judy I've never had to close a play under these circumstances before.

Justin I don't suppose any of us have. Comedians talk of dying on stage but they don't mean literally!

Judy Poor Millie!

Justin (*leaving his task and strolling DR*) It's been an ordeal for all of us.

Judy I can't believe it's happened. It's strange because though I've never seen anyone dead before, I knew right away that she was—that Millie was dead.

Justin Not all that surprising considering the mess her face was in! (*He goes to help her, handing her clothes off the clothes rail*)

Judy Yes, it was horrid, wasn't it? (*She inspects the clothes he hands her to look for any necessary repairs*) When that doctor came on stage he said to cover up her face and I couldn't find anything at first—it was such a mess anyway, and then Pearl came on and gave me her scarf. I thought that was decent of her. She looked terrible, didn't she? Pearl, I mean. She went quite green. I thought she was going to faint!

Justin I thought *I* was going to faint! *You* seemed to bear up all right.

Judy I have a strong stomach. I had to have. I was the one who cleared up the bits splattered all over the scenery ... oh, sorry, perhaps that was a touch insensitive.

Justin It was rather—I suggest you don't say anything like that in front of Addie.

Judy No, I wouldn't. I realize somebody had to do the clearing up. In a way it's been quite useful for me all this happening, because I want to write and all's grist to the mill for a writer. Now I can write about violent death. For one thing I know that brains really do look like cold porridge.

Justin Judy—please—I'm not squeamish, but really there are some things you don't talk about.

Judy Sorry! I'm afraid I speak without thinking sometimes.

Justin It's much better to think without speaking!

Judy Point taken!

Justin What are you going to do after this? Have you a job lined up?

Judy No—I'll be out of work again.

Justin One gets used to it in this game, the uncertainty from job to job.

(*Wearying of helping her, he wanders* DR)

Judy continues with her packing, dragging shoes etc. from behind the screen and putting them in another box

Judy It doesn't worry me. My whole life has been uncertain. I don't think I could bear security. It would be so dull.

Justin Life in the theatre is never dull! That's a fact. You've got a place in London, haven't you? Somewhere to go?

Judy I have, but even that doesn't bother me, either. A cardboard box under the arches would suit me if I didn't have anything else, just sit there waiting for people to feel sorry for me. I know a chap with a Ph.D. who makes more money begging than working.

Justin That can't be true!

Judy It is—and he doesn't seem to mind, either. He hates being organized, you see, as I do.

Justin Yes, I have noticed!

Judy (*defensively*) But, Justin, I was improving, wasn't I? That is until the other night. (*She stops her packing*) You're not blaming me for the accident, are you? I know I didn't check the gun before she went on, but after all, it had been locked up since the previous performance. There was a box of blanks but no real bullets. At least that's what I thought.

Justin Then how did it happen?

Judy (*miserably*) I don't know. I told the police all I knew. They can't blame me. It must have been an accident. What else?

Justin Of course it was an accident. Anything else is unthinkable.

Judy What do you mean? Anything else? You don't think she did it deliberately, do you?

Justin Millie was a bit scatty but even she wouldn't want to go out in quite such a dramatic style. Besides she couldn't be sure it would kill her. It might just have ruined her looks. She'd hardly want to do that!

Judy No, of course not. Neither would anyone else.

Justin gives her a sharp look

Just want to ruin her looks, I mean.

Addie enters

Addie Oh hallo, Justin—hallo, Judy—it's good of you to clear up for me. I left everything in such a mess on Thursday.

Justin Hi! (*He goes up and kisses her on the cheek*)

Judy Hallo, Addie. I was thinking about the costumes for Nathan's—we don't want to pay for another week.

Addie You are sensible! (*She sits down heavily at her dressing-table and sighs*) I don't seem to be able to get myself together at all. I can't think properly.

Justin It's the shock!

Addie I can't get her out of my mind—poor Millie. (*Her voice breaks*)

Justin It's been a bad time for all of us. (*He motions to Judy to go*) You can leave that for now, dear.

Judy (*taking the hint*) Oh yes, I've got something to do backstage. (*She goes over to Addie. Earnestly*) I'm so sorry, Addie, about everything. I liked her too—I liked Millie. We all did. She was so full of life and vivacity, the last person one would expect... I mean, you don't think she would do it deliberately, do you?

Addie Do what?

Justin (*sharply*) That's enough, Judy—thanks!

Judy All right. I'm going. See you later.

Judy goes off

Addie Thank you, Justin. (*She sniffs and wipes her eyes*) I didn't really feel I could cope with her chatter at the moment. What did she mean—do it deliberately. Millie? Commit suicide? That's the last thing she'd do.

Justin Of course, it would be.

Addie Like Judy said, Millie was so full of life... (*Her voice breaks*)

Justin There, there, don't think about it! We must have a talk about other things. After all, life goes on!

Addie (*sniffing*) Yes, you're right. We have to talk. (*She dries her eyes and consults her image in the mirror*)

Justin What are we going to do?

Addie Apart from what we have done, you mean?

Justin I hate giving money back. We've had people at the box office all day coming for their money back, those who know about it, but there are some who don't. I was almost tempted to go up, after all...

Addie No, it would be too insensitive after what's happened. I couldn't bear it.

Justin Oh yes, you're right. It's too late now, anyway, we're half packed, but knowing how ghoulish the public are we might just have had great business for a couple of nights once the story got round. We still have to pay the cast till next week, don't forget!

Addie I can't think about practicalities at the moment. I just don't care. I've lost my best friend! (*Her voice breaks*)

Justin (*cynically*) Your best friend and you hated her!

Addie I didn't—not at all!

Justin Sorry—didn't mean it.

Addie We had our ups and downs—who doesn't? She was a bitch at times, but we had a lot in common.

Justin Yes, I noticed. How did your mutual husband take it—the accident?

Addie He was shocked, naturally. He was very fond of Millie, in his own way.

Justin (*relaxing on the settee*) At least he wasn't grilled by the police like I was—nearly two hours!

Addie I thought you just gave a statement—like I did.

Justin (*peevishly*) It felt like a grilling. You'd think I'd killed the silly woman—I mean poor woman.

Addie I had to give a statement as well. It was awful. I just couldn't explain why I hadn't given the gun back the night before. But it was locked in my drawer. Nobody else had access to it but me. I just can't understand how it happened. I mean it was supposed to be firing blanks.

Justin That was the puzzling thing. Who put the live bullet in the gun—and why?

Addie It was just an accident. It had to be.

Justin I suppose so. But where did the live bullet come from in the first place?

Addie How do I know? It must have been in the box with the blanks. What other explanation is there? Nobody would want to kill Millie. She was perfectly sweet!

Justin Addie—darling, if you could hear yourself!

Addie Well, she was. In her own way. Not to everyone's taste. She drank like a fish and she was a veritable man-eater, but still she was my friend. (*Her voice breaks again*)

Justin (*ignoring her grief*) A tragic accident. That's what it said in the paper. Did you see it? We were in the *Daily Mirror*. "Tragic Accident as Understudy Takes on Star Role"—that's what it said.

Addie Who on earth told them?

Justin I did, of course. There's no such thing as bad publicity, darling.

Addie Ah, well, it's true anyway. That's what it was, a tragic, terrible accident! (*She sniffles and takes a tissue from her dressing-table*)

Justin watches with cynical disinterest and then makes his way over to her

Justin There is one thing you can derive some comfort from...

Addie (*sniffing and mopping her eyes*) What do you mean? How can there be? What possible comfort could there be now? (*She meets his gaze suspiciously*)

Justin (*with smug confidence*) There is the little matter of the insurance, darling.

Addie What insurance?

Justin There's a clause in our insurance policy. Sudden death causing closure means we can recoup the costs of the tour. You must have known.

Addie (*almost in a panic*) No, I didn't know, or if I did I'd forgotten. You're not suggesting that I would deliberately kill my best friend... (*Her voice breaks*)

Justin I'm not suggesting anything, darling, but it is convenient, isn't it? A bonus in a way.

Addie A bonus?

Justin You have lost your best friend, as you say—but before you were facing bankruptcy and now you're not. That has to be a bonus!

Addie I—I don't look at it like that. I only know Millie's dead and I miss her!

Justin Still it must be a relief that you are not broke, after all—I must admit I wasn't looking forward to selling my flat and being homeless.

Addie (*confused*) I didn't know about the insurance, or if I did, I'd forgotten. I'm so forgetful these days.

Justin I wouldn't have described you as forgetful, not at all. Still, as long as the police don't think it odd, what does it matter?

Addie The police? Why should the police think anything at all? Why should they have to know?

Justin Exactly what I feel—why should they have to know?

Pause

Ed enters

Ed The stage door was open...
Justin Yes—we're just clearing up.
Ed You said you'd be here, Addie. I wondered if I could help. I was worried about you.
Addie (*going up to him and embracing him*) How sweet of you! You don't know how glad I am to see you! Justin has just been accusing me of murdering Millie.
Justin It wasn't an accusation—nothing like it.
Addie That's what it sounded like.
Ed You can't be serious!
Justin I was just floating a thought...
Addie Well, float it elsewhere!

Justin exits, looking peeved

Ed What's come over him? He wasn't serious, was he?
Addie I don't know I'm sure. I suppose he's just fed up like the rest of us because the show's folded.
Ed Still, there's no need to make accusations like that.

They both go and sit on the settee

Addie That's what I thought. He claims we have an insurance policy that covers our losses if a member of the cast suffers sudden death. I didn't know about it. Or if I did I'd forgotten.
Ed I've never heard of such insurance cover. Actors would be bumped off all over the place if that were so!
Addie It is quite a motive for murder.
Ed Ridiculous. Anyway, if it were so—what about him? He'd invested in this play as well, hadn't he?
Addie That's what I thought. Oh, I don't know why we're talking like this. I don't want to talk about it. I'm so fed up!
Ed What are you going to do now?
Addie (*rising and going back to the dressing-table*) Pack up and go home, what else? I still can't get over it. Poor Millie! How could Justin say—what he said? He knew I was very fond of Millie. (*She looks in the mirror*) Look at me! Don't I look a mess? I've hardly slept for two nights. I hate it when I get bags under my eyes.
Ed That tragic air rather suits you.
Addie (*brightening*) Does it? Oh, you are a darling!
Ed I've been thinking—that's why I wanted to see you today, what about my

play, now you're free? After all, an Edward Gibb production is not to be sniffed at.

Addie (*joining him*) Darling, I don't want to hurt your feelings, but you're going back twenty years. Nowadays all they want in the West End are lavish musicals or old actresses taking their clothes off.

Ed I can't manage a lavish musical but I could easily write in a nude scene—why not?

Addie I positively refuse to take my clothes off.

Ed I haven't actually asked you.

Addie Just in case you do. Anyway if it's the play you were talking about with the two mature actresses sparring away—how on earth would you fit in a nude scene? Unless you intend them to be gay?

Ed No, that's stretching it a bit, but I could easily write something in. Involvement with a young actor.

Addie That's impossible. Most of them *are* gay.

Ed Or a stage hand or something.

Addie That is the silliest thing I ever heard in my life. You'd never get away with it. Nobody wants salacious sex. It must be an integral part of the plot.

Ed All right. I give up. Sexy stuff is not my style, but I still think my play would stand a chance with you in it.

Addie Well, darling, I won't say I'm not tempted, but how can we finance it? Even if Justin is right about the insurance, all it will do is keep me afloat. I daren't re-mortgage my house again, darling. I've learned my lesson with this play. This was to be my comeback. I gambled and lost. I can't go through that anxiety again. Next time I'll be the one to shoot myself—oh, I didn't mean that! What is the matter with me?

Ed You're upset—we all are, and I know how you feel. But I seriously thought you might invest in my play, just for old times' sake! After all, I was somebody when I met you...

Addie Yes, and when you left me I became somebody, but that's a long time ago. I've made and lost a small fortune since then.

Ed So what happens now? Here we are both hoping to get something out of one another and having nothing to give.

Addie That's the story of my life.

There is a knock at the door and Judy enters

Judy Justin wondered if you'd like a cup of tea. I'm making one.

Addie Yes, darling, I would—what about you, Ed?

Ed If you have nothing stronger.

Judy No, we haven't. Addie, I must say how sorry I am about everything. I should have checked the gun before Millie took it. Will you ever forgive me?

Addie Of course. It was an accident.
Judy I shall never forget it as long as I live. I expect I'll write about it some day to erase it from my memory. Writing is therapy. All the best writers say so. I'll never forget the look on her face when I picked her up——
Addie We really would like that cup of tea, darling...
Judy Yes—of course, and I will have to send off those costumes today. Let me know when it's convenient.
Addie I surely will.

Judy exits

Ed I don't know how she could see the look on Millie's face when it was covered in blood, the half that was still there anyway!
Addie Please don't!
Ed I suppose she's just being dramatic. We theatricals all tend to dramatise, don't we? Can't resist a good yarn.
Addie You mean Millie's death—a good yarn?
Ed Sorry—I didn't mean that the way it sounded. Callous!
Addie It's all right, I understand. None of us are functioning rationally. It's been such a shock. And, after all, it has closed the play.

Pearl enters

Pearl Hallo, darlings, Justin said you were here. I came back to pack. Isn't it sad? I still can't believe it. When's the funeral? I shall go.
Addie Oh Pearl!

Pearl and Addie collapse in tears. Ed watches them—rather bemused

Ed Nothing like a good cry for relieving tension!
Addie (*wiping her eyes*) How cynical you are, Ed!
Pearl (*with deep insincerity*) I'll miss her. I know we had our differences but deep down we both respected one another. She was a good actress, under-used, misunderstood, but still she had talent.
Addie Perhaps you'd like to say a few words at the funeral, dear, it's quite the fashion these days.
Pearl Oh, no, I couldn't possibly. I'd break down.
Ed You could act it, act not breaking down.
Pearl No, I couldn't. I'm not a good enough actress for that. I feel so guilty. I wish I hadn't upstaged her like that. I did it deliberately.
Ed All's fair in love and acting, dear.
Pearl I was so annoyed about the way she behaved with Guy. He is my only son, and he's so bright. I didn't want him tarnished by her.

Ed What a lovely metaphor—may I use it in my play?
Pearl What? Oh, of course, use anything. What play?
Ed The play I wrote for Millie and Addie—now only for Addie I fear! If only
   I had a backer.
Pearl Is there a part for me? I'd love to be in your play.
Ed What?
Pearl I mean without Millie, wouldn't I do? I know I'm a bit older.
Ed (*decisively*) Yes, you are.
Pearl I have some money I'd love to invest.
Ed (*with a quick glance at Addie*) Age doesn't matter at all.
Addie Of course not.

*Addie quickly crosses to her side, so that Pearl is between Addie and Ed, front
of stage*

Ed How much?
Pearl What?
Ed How much——
Addie Money?
Pearl Quite a lot. My late husband was in oil.
Addie How messy! I mean how great. I had no idea you were well off,
   darling. I mean, why bother to work?
Pearl I love work. I love the theatre. And I'm lonely at home in a great big
   mansion.
Ed A great big mansion!
Pearl Well, quite big. Modestly big. Fifty rooms. But of course we only use
   a little bit of it now. I hate rattling around in a place like that all on my own.
   It makes me feel so small.

Addie and Ed exchange glances of amazement

  Judy enters, bringing in two cups of tea on a tray

Judy The sugar's in the bowl. Hope that's all right.
Addie Thank you, dear.
Judy (*putting the tray down on Addie's dressing-table* R) Oh, Pearl's here
   as well. Would you like a cuppa?
Pearl No, I'm just leaving.
Addie Don't go yet...
Ed No—don't go!
Pearl I must pack my things, and I'm sure I have an outfit to return to
   Nathan's.
Judy I'll help you. (*She goes round the back of the settee to* DL) I know
   everyone wants to get out of here—the atmosphere is awful.

Ed Do you mean creepy?
Judy No, not just creepy. Apprehensive.
Ed Apprehensive? An apprehensive atmosphere? How do you account for that?
Judy Because it isn't finished, is it? The story isn't finished.
Ed What story?
Judy What happened to Millie—it won't be over until we know why.
Addie We might never know why.
Judy But we must. (*In rising hysteria*) Don't you see? We must know why—or else I shall feel guilty for the rest of my life. I shall always think it was my fault.
Ed (*soothing her*) It wasn't your fault at all.
Judy It was awful! I've never seen anyone dead before. (*She starts weeping*) I still can't believe it.
Addie Don't upset yourself. You mustn't feel guilty. We all know it was an accident.
Judy It must have been. But the police asked me such a lot of questions. They seemed to think it was odd that it should happen when it was your understudy going on and not you. I explained that you had a terrible migraine.
Addie I explained too.
Judy It just seemed odd to them, such a coincidence.
Addie Of course it would seem odd to them. The police have no imagination.
Ed What about you, Pearl? Did they question you?
Pearl Only briefly. After all I wasn't on the stage when it happened. I never have anything to do with the gun. What could I tell them?
Ed Now, if the police had the imagination of a playwright they would pick the most unlikely person and grill them all the more.
Pearl The unlikely person being me?
Ed I think so—don't you?
Pearl (*alarmed*) But I don't think I am unlikely. It was no secret I didn't get on with Millie.
Ed Not enough to kill her?
Pearl Certainly not!
Addie (*sharply*) This really is a silly conversation. Nobody killed Millie. It was an accident.
Judy (*tragically*) It was all my fault! (*She sobs*)
Pearl (*crossing to her*) Now, now, nobody blames you. Come on, let's get everything cleared up and we can go home.
Judy (*collapsing against Pearl, sobbing*) I don't want to go home. I don't know what I'm going to do. I don't want to be alone. I don't want to think!
Pearl Oh, you'll be all right—we'll sort something out. (*She begins to move towards the door, her arm around Judy*)

Ed Don't go, Pearl—we must talk.
Addie Yes, darling—so much to talk about...
Pearl I won't be long...

Pearl goes off with her arm around Judy's shoulders, comforting her

Left alone, Addie and Ed exchange delighted glances. Then Addie crosses to Ed with the two mugs of tea, and they sit on the settee

Addie What do you think?
Ed It's a possibility!
Addie Will she invest?
Ed Offer her a part—she's bound to.
Addie But she's got a part—in this...
Ed You're surely not thinking of asking her to invest in this load of rubbish?
Addie (*hurt*) It crossed my mind.
Ed Don't be daft, Addie. We'll get her to invest in mine—offer her the part I was going to give Millie.
Addie (*doubtfully*) Do you think she can do it?
Ed Who cares, as long as she puts up the ackers?
Addie I care. I don't want my name associated with a failure.
Ed Don't you mean—with another failure?
Addie Perhaps I do.
Ed Don't you see—this saves our bacon? All of us!
Addie Except Millie.
Ed It's too late for Millie. Anyway, if this hadn't happened we'd never have known about Pearl's millions.
Addie We still don't know if it's millions.
Ed Why should she lie? But I'm surprised at you. Fancy not finding out before!
Addie (*rising irritably, and going to the dressing-table*) I don't go round asking my cast if they were ever married to a millionaire, do I? It isn't the sort of question that springs to mind when you're casting a play.
Ed Perhaps it should. In future I shall make a point of it.

Pearl enters

Pearl The poor little thing is quite upset—understandably of course, but it wasn't her fault. I don't suppose anyone will ever know how a real bullet came to be put in that gun. It's a mystery.
Ed Speaking of mysteries, that's what my play is, a mystery.
Pearl Oh, yes, we were talking about it, weren't we? Before Judy came in.
Ed The thing is there's a simply marvellous part for someone like you.

Pearl (*thrilled*) Someone like me?
Ed Yes—I thought of casting you and Addie—both marvellous parts!
Pearl You mean the part you were going to give Millie?
Ed You could do it just as well.
Pearl Are you sure? How marvellous! (*She embraces him with enthusiasm*)
Ed (*disentangling himself*) Yes—I'm sure. I thought of you when I saw you
  in this but by then I'd already promised it to Millie.
Addie So Pearl has a motive for murder?
Pearl (*in a slight panic*) Oh dear! Oh no! I didn't know about it, did I? Not
  before—what happened to Millie!
Addie Of course not, silly. I didn't mean it! I've played in so many crummy
  thrillers I even think like one. Now, perhaps we should go and talk this over
  at lunch somewhere.
Ed Good idea!
Pearl I've still got some things to pack.
Addie Leave them for now. I've got loads to do as well but I don't feel like
  it. Let's go across to *The New Inn* and talk things over.
Ed Yes, come along, Pearl, dear. We can have a nice chat.
Pearl Oh, yes, I'd like that. I was wondering what to do for the rest of the day,
  and with no show tonight either.
Addie We won't be long, but I could do with a drink and a spot of lunch. (*She
  looks in the mirror*) I left home this morning without any breakfast. I seem
  to be in a complete flat spin at the moment. Do I look all right?
Ed (*addressing Addie's reflection*) Gorgeous, darling! Oh, God, I was
  speaking to your reflection. I got told off for doing that to Millie the other
  night.
Addie And then she died! How ominous, darling! It's a good job I'm not
  superstitious!
Pearl I won't be sorry to leave this theatre now, though—will you?
Addie To be honest—no. I'll be glad.

They are ready to leave

Justin enters

Justin Oh—were you going somewhere?
Addie Just for a spot of lunch, we're all famished.
Justin Could I have a word—Addie—do you mind?
Addie (*after a moment's hesitation*) No, that's all right. You go on—you
  two. I'll join you shortly.
Justin Perhaps we both will.
Addie (*reluctantly*) Yes, why not?
Ed OK—come along, Pearl. Let's go and have a chat. I'll tell you about the
  play...

Pearl I'm longing to hear about it.

Pearl and Ed go off, talking as they go

Justin What play is that they're talking about?
Addie Ed's new play. It seems that our Pearl actually has a few bob! We're hoping to get her to invest.
Justin That's marvellous!
Addie He actually wrote it for Millie and me...
Justin It's an ill wind that blows nobody any good!
Addie That is rather flippant, Justin, if you're referring to the death of my friend!
Justin I'm sure I didn't mean to offend you.
Addie (*stiffly*) It doesn't matter! What did you want—I'm keen to join them. I'm hungry!
Justin Funny, isn't it, how sorrow doesn't rob one of one's appetite!
Addie (*furiously*) Will you stop making these horrible innuendos! I can't help being hungry. It won't help Millie if I starve myself, will it? Now what did you want me for?
Justin What we were talking about—before.
Addie Now you're being cryptic.
Justin The insurance angle.
Addie I told Ed—he doesn't believe it! He doesn't believe there was such an insurance clause.
Justin Call my bluff! Find out!
Addie I might just do that.
Justin The police are most anxious to find a motive if they decide Millie was murdered after all.
Addie She wasn't——
Justin How can we be sure? The only thing we can be sure of is that the gun was in your possession until you gave it to Millie. Nobody else had access to it. And Millie only went on because *you* felt ill. Anybody can fake a migraine—especially a consummate actress like yourself.

Addie is about to reply

I'm not saying it *is* what happened, I'm saying it could be!
Addie It's all nonsense!
Justin Then there is your pretence of liking Millie which could quite easily hide a deep hatred. After all, she did steal your man.
Addie That was so long ago, years and years ago, I'd forgiven her—forgiven them both!
Justin Oh, I know. I understand. I knew you were good friends now. I'm just

saying what it could look like to the police if they were in possession of all
the facts.

Addie (*after a moment*) So—what is it you want?

Justin Not much! A job.

Addie We all do...

Justin This new play of Ed's—you'll need a company manager.

Addie That will be up to Ed.

Justin But you have so much influence over him, haven't you?

Addie (*after a moment*) All right. I'll see what I can do. Is there anything else?

Justin Not at the moment—go and have your lunch.

Addie I seem to have lost my appetite. Still, I'll go and join them. I'll be back
later—please remind Judy about the costumes, won't you?

Justin Surely.

Addie (*about to leave*) I want you to know something, Justin.

Justin Yes?

Addie I never liked you and now I know why. You're a shit!

Addie glares at him and walks off

Justin stands smiling, looking after her as——

——the CURTAIN *falls*

SCENE 2

The same. Later

*The clothes rail has disappeared behind the screen together with most of the
clothes*

*Judy is packing an evening dress into a large cardboard box on the settee.
She has tissue paper, string and a large pair of scissors*

Addie enters. She is flushed from a good lunch and a few drinks

Addie Oh, you still here? I thought you'd be finished by now. We were so
long, dawdling over lunch.

Judy It's all right. This is the last one. All the rest are in the hamper behind
the screen all ready to go. This dress was just too delicate to crush up in a
hamper.

Addie You are a dear. I simply hate packing after a show. It's so boring.

Judy It's sad, too, isn't it? The company breaking up? That is, unless you
have something else to look forward to.

Addie Ah, but we have, you see! It appears we're much too involved to break up. A nest of vipers we may be but at least we all know it! God—my head! Don't say I'm getting another migraine.

Judy I'm percolating some coffee. I'll get it. I could do with a cup. I always keep some on the go when I'm busy packing. Would you like a cup?

Addie Thanks—p'raps I will. I left before having any coffee and the wine has made me feel quite sleepy.

Judy I'll get it.

Judy goes off

Addie on her own starts clearing out the drawers of her dressing-table. She comes across some old photographs and looks at them

Judy enters with coffee in a percolator and two mugs

I know how you like it—strong, black and sweet.

Addie That's right! (*She blows her nose and dabs at her eyes*)

Judy (*putting down the tray on the dressing-table*) Is anything wrong?

Addie Some photographs here of Millie and myself when we first met—I found them at home and brought them in. Only last week we were laughing about them—the way we both tried to be in the height of fashion and now they look so dreadfully dated. Poor Millie! (*She sniffs*) I can't believe she's dead!

Judy I expect you miss her—knowing her for so long.

Addie I miss her more than I thought possible.

Judy I know how you feel. I had a girlfriend who died of a drug overdose when she was sixteen. I still think about her even now. She was the only real friend I've ever had.

Addie That's a shame! Still, it's no good either of us dwelling on the past, is it? I know Millie wouldn't expect me to mope. Life goes on. (*She dries her eyes and helps herself to coffee, pouring one for Judy*)

Judy I suppose it depends what you have to look forward to. (*She takes her coffee but doesn't drink it*)

Addie (*spooning sugar into her mug*) Yes, I'm lucky. Ed has a new play coming out. That's what we've been celebrating, actually.

Judy Mr Gibb has a new play? How exciting! What's it about?

Addie Two middle-aged actresses—one of whom is murdered and suspicion falls on the other one.

Judy A bit of a coincidence.

Addie (*sharply*) What do you mean?

Judy You know—what's happened here...

Addie There's no parallel. Millie wasn't murdered, and I certainly didn't murder her.

Judy (*flustered*) Of course not—I didn't mean that. I just meant that the play is about two actresses and one dies, that's all. (*She takes her coffee over to the dressing-table* L *and begins to pack Millie's things in a box*) Does someone die on stage in this new play, or what happens?

Addie (*disgruntled*) I haven't read it yet so I have no idea. Like all playwrights, Ed likes to keep everything under wraps until the last minute. I think he's afraid someone will steal his plot.

Judy I know how he feels. I want to be a writer some day, and I shall be like that—jealous of my ideas, possessive of my characters and I certainly won't want to discuss the plot until I'm sure about it.

Addie, relaxing a little, takes her coffee over to the settee and sits

Addie What do you want to write, plays—or something more serious, like the Great British Novel?

Judy I don't know yet. P'raps I'll write both, but they will be thrillers. I've made up my mind about that. Thrillers or ghost stories.

Addie (*yawning*) You like creepy stuff?

Judy I do rather. When I was a little girl I used to read the ghost stories of M. R. James to get to sleep.

Addie Good heavens, reading ghost stories to get to sleep! I should have thought they would be guaranteed to keep you awake.

Judy Not in my case—reality to me was much more horrific.

Addie How odd! (*She sips her coffee*) This is good! You certainly know how to make good coffee. You're not bad backstage either—except for the flapping. But that comes with experience—being able to keep your cool.

Judy I suppose so. Justin is a good example. He's taught me a lot. I'd love to work with him again. Is he going to be company manager for Mr Gibb's new play?

Addie Did he say he was?

Judy Sort of.

Addie I suppose he is then—where is he by the way? Eavesdropping at the door?

Judy You sound as if you don't like him!

Addie I love him! Where is he?

Judy He left a note on the main door to say the show was cancelled and how to get their money back and then as far as I know he went.

Addie He went?

Judy Back to town.

Addie He might have said goodbye.

Judy He said he'd be in touch.

Addie I'm sure he will. Anyway, he needn't get too excited about Ed's play. It hasn't got off the ground yet, it all depends on Pearl's millions.

Judy Pearl's millions! (*Doubtfully*) Do you think she's got millions?

Addie She says she has.

Judy She talked about her manor house and all that, did she?

Addie Oh, you know about it. Apparently, her late husband was something big in oil.

Judy Sounds like a sardine!

Addie That's what I thought.

Judy He might have left her a few bob but I doubt she's got any now.

Addie (*alarmed*) What makes you think that?

Judy I got to know Guy—her son—quite well. You must remember him?

Addie I do—Pearl was worried about Millie chasing him.

Judy She needn't have been. He isn't interested in women.

Addie How did you find that out?

Judy The usual way!

Addie I see. And he told you Pearl hadn't got any money?

Judy She did have at one time. Guy soon got through it after his old man died. I think Pearl is like the rest of us—struggling to exist!

Addie (*upset*) If that's true—oh God, poor old Ed! Poor old me! Oh, shit! I'm really fed up now!

Judy Sorry to break the news.

Addie How could she take us in like that? (*She rises from the settee*) I'd better go across and break the news to Ed before he starts booking theatres and things.

Judy (*quickly*) No, don't go yet. Let's clear up and we can both go over. She's more likely to admit it if I'm with you.

Addie Yes—you're probably right. Let poor old Ed live in his fool's paradise for a bit longer. Oh, shit, shit, shit!

Judy I know how you feel!

Addie You don't—you can't possibly know!

Judy I was hoping for work as well. I could do with it.

Addie We all could.

Judy I'll get something. It's usually easier to get backstage than acting. I've never worried about acting. My mother was an actress, you see. It rather put me off.

Addie Oh, why?

Judy She was so busy—I never saw her.

Addie It is a demanding profession. I could do with some more coffee. I feel so sleepy. Too much wine. (*She pours herself some more coffee*) I don't know what I'm going to do now. Justin told me there was insurance to cover our losses, I only hope he was telling the truth, otherwise I'm really broke, but then so is he! God, how could I get to my age and do what I've done and end up with nothing—in fact with debts? It's bloody ridiculous!

Judy It's bad luck. You don't deserve it. You've had quite an illustrious career. I know because I've followed it with great interest.

Addie (*moving back to sit on the settee with her coffee*) How sweet of you, dear! That's rather flattering!

Judy It was inevitable really. Once I knew who you were.

Addie (*puzzled*) Knew who I was?

Judy (*leaving what she is doing*) I followed your career because you reminded me of someone I used to know. I hadn't any real prototype, no real mother, so in a way I invented one. She was glamorous, beautiful, self-assured, all the things I was not. Sometimes I would look for this prototype in my foster mothers, but she was never there. And I could never conform to the sort of child they wanted me to be. They tried so hard. My longest placement was with a couple who tried very hard to make me conform.

Addie They weren't cruel, were they? I hate that—to hear about such things!

Judy To their own lights they weren't cruel. They wanted to improve me, that's all. They never hit me or anything like that but they were very strict. All my misdemeanours were recorded in a punishment book with the date. The punishment I hated most of all was writing a hundred lines of "I must obey my parents". Because I knew very well they were not my parents.

Addie It must have been awful for you.

Judy It was. I ran away and kept on running. It was no good, wherever they placed me I was always unhappy, always rebellious, different homes, different schools, different parents—none of them *mine*!

Addie (*nervously, embarrassed by these revelations*) It's strange, isn't it, the way we work together while we're doing a play every night and yet never really know one another?

Judy That suited me really, the anonymity. I liked nobody knowing about me.

Addie It's not that we weren't interested.

Judy (*scoffing*) It's just that you weren't interested.

Addie No, that's not true! The play is always more important.

Judy (*sarcastically*) Of course, make-believe is always more important than reality, all theatricals know that! (*Abruptly*) Did you have any children, Addie?

Addie (*stiffly*) No, I didn't have time. I was too busy with my career.

Judy My foster mothers now, they never had careers. Their careers were caring for other people's children.

Addie That's admirable, of course. To each his own!

Judy Ah yes—their *own*, but they weren't their *own*, those children. Do you think it's possible to love other people's children like your own?

Addie I have no idea. That is one subject on which I must plead complete ignorance.

Judy It would have been all right, you see, if my mother, my real mother, had agreed that I should be adopted. But she would never give her consent, so I had to be fostered, time and time again, a succession of different parents, all pretending to care about me when I knew they didn't, couldn't care about me, not as I wanted to be cared about. When I was sixteen I ran away for the last time, with my friend, the friend who died. She helped me look for my real mother.

Addie (*apprehensively*) What happened?

Judy We found her. I wrote her a letter. But she didn't want to know about me. She had her career to think about. I was apparently an embarrassment to her. Then my friend died and for a while I didn't care about anything else. (*She pauses*) It would make a good play—don't you think?

Addie Only if it had a strong ending.

Judy It has—a very strong ending.

Addie (*nervously*) I thought I heard the stage door. Did you hear it—do you think they're coming back?

Judy No, they're not coming back. The stage door is locked. We are alone—Mother.

Addie Don't call me that! It isn't true!

Judy Do you deny that you ever had a child? Do you deny it?

Addie No—I don't deny it—there was a child, but that doesn't mean the child grew up to be you! I don't believe it.

Judy What happened to your child?

Addie She was fostered—she was adopted—I'm not sure.

Judy You're not sure! Your own child! You're not sure!

Addie You're very judgemental. You don't understand. I was young, hard-up and struggling with my career, I couldn't bring up a child. How could I?

Judy So you abandoned me?

Addie It wasn't you. I don't believe that!

Judy I wrote to you when I was sixteen, don't you remember? I desperately needed help.

Addie I was always getting begging letters in those days. I was usually most generous. I expect I sent you some money.

Judy You sent me a hundred pounds. A hundred pounds for a ruined life!

Addie I don't accept that. I don't accept that you're my responsibility. I didn't—don't believe you're anything to do with me.

Judy I could prove it. I could embarrass you by proving it. My birth certificate bears your real name. Annie March. That's your real name, isn't it? Not Adelaide Marchbanks.

Addie You could have stolen it. You can't prove that you are the same child—my child.

Judy DNA testing could prove it.

Pause

Addie What is it you want? I haven't any money—not much anyway.

Judy I don't want money.

Addie What then?

Judy I want revenge—that's my strong ending.

Addie Oh, do stop! I feel so odd. My head is spinning. Too much wine—and you're upsetting me! I feel terrible.

Judy Take some deep breaths. You'll be all right. There was a sedative in your coffee. Just a little one. So that you wouldn't run away. So that you'd listen to me.

Addie I'd listen anyway. Why shouldn't I? You haven't any right to do this—to—to drug me. I don't understand.

Judy I think you do. I think you do understand. You should have listened to me before, when I was destitute at sixteen, homeless, walking the streets, begging, the daughter of a rich and famous actress, destitute and begging.

Addie (*weakly*) I was at the peak of my career. I couldn't throw it all away on a mistake.

Judy A mistake! Yes, I was a mistake! You should have had me aborted.

Addie I didn't believe in abortion.

Judy Just abandonment, I see. Very responsible, I'm sure! Well, I haven't the same scruples. (*She picks up the scissors left lying on the settee*)

Addie What do you mean?

Judy I can't forgive you, you see. I can't bear to think of you living, breathing, being alive, enjoying life. I want to rid the world of you, and that's what I'm going to do. (*She holds the scissors in her hand menacingly*)

Addie You can't——

Judy (*leaning over her, the scissors poised at her neck*) What's to stop me?

Addie I'll scream—I'll get help.

Judy Nobody will hear you. We're alone. Are you scared? I hope you are. I hope you're scared.

Addie (*cowering before her*) Please don't hurt me...

Judy Look at you! Where's all your confidence now? Where is the famous actress now, so self-assured, so full of conceit? (*She relaxes her grip and stands back*) No, I'm not going to do it that way. I just wanted to see your reaction. I wanted to make you beg!

Addie (*with relief*) Oh Judy, think what you're doing. Think about yourself. Think about your own life!

Judy My life? What do you care for my life? You never have.

Addie (*in genuine contrition*) I'm sorry. I didn't understand. Oh Judy, dear, you surely don't want to kill me. You just meant to frighten me, that's it, isn't it?

Judy (*she crosses to the dressing-table* L *and lays down the scissors*) You haven't worked it out yet, have you? I always meant to kill you, but it's too quick and simple for you to die without knowing why. I would be robbed of my revenge. You have to know the reason, you see. (*She pauses*) That's why I put a real bullet in the gun.

Addie (*intrigued, despite her fear*) You killed Millie by mistake?
Judy Of course not. It was all part of the plot. I had the means, the gun, I had the victim, Millie, and I had the suspect, you. (*She moves around the settee, never far from Addie*)

Addie watches her like a rabbit watching a cobra

I'd kept trying to find ways to keep you off the stage so that Millie took your part. I've sabotaged the play as much as I could. I was getting a bit desperate about things with only a week to go and then you suffered one of your famous migraines—and my chance was presented to me. It was easy to dupe Millie. I took the gun from her in the wings on the pretext of checking it over and slipped the real bullet into the breach. Millie had to die, you see, and suspicion had to fall on you.
Addie But it hasn't. I don't think it has.
Judy It will—when they find you dead, after you kill yourself in a fit of remorse.
Addie But I wouldn't do that. I won't! (*She tries to struggle up from the settee, but collapses back*) I feel as weak as a kitten!
Judy You are! That's what you are. A kitten not a cat. (*The pace quickens— she is business-like now, as she crosses to the dressing-table*) This is the scenario. Remorse has overtaken you—you killed your best friend whom you had never forgiven for taking your husband all those years ago. You killed her and tried to make it look as if you yourself were the victim. (*She picks up a large syringe from the dressing-table*) Then overcome with remorse you decide to take the easy way out. (*She displays the syringe checking that it is full, held to the light*) A peaceful slumber, the best and the most peaceful you will ever have, drifting away on a pink cloud to eternity. (*She crosses to the settee*)
Addie (*shrinking from her*) What's that in your hand? What is in that thing?
Judy Pure heroin. It will be a peaceful death. Some people might envy you. (*She grasps Addie's arm and pushes back her sleeve*)
Addie (*struggling*) Don't be so stupid ... you'll never get away with it.
Judy I think I will. There is nothing to link you and me. You so cleverly covered your tracks. Why should anyone see a connection between us? Even if they did—why should I kill you? Nobody knows the hell my life has been! Nobody knows how much I hate you!
Addie Judy, please don't! You can't really mean to kill me. I don't believe it.
Judy You will. (*She is about to plunge the needle in her arm*)
Addie Don't!

Justin enters

Justin No—Judy—don't!

Judy (*stopping in confusion*) Where did you come from? I thought you'd left.

Justin (*urgently but still in control*) That's what I meant you to think. In fact, I was listening backstage.

Judy (*moving away from Addie*) Listening!

Justin I rigged up the intercom so that I could hear what was going on.

Judy You could hear...?

Justin That's right. I was hoping Addie would give herself away, instead of which you did. I set a trap but caught a different bird—a rather deadly one as it turned out!

Addie You didn't trust me—oh Justin—how could you?

Justin (*not taking his eyes off Judy*) I'm sorry, Addie, I thought you'd killed Millie but I couldn't work out the motive—so I made up the insurance story to gauge your reaction.

Addie You made it up—there isn't any insurance?

Justin I'm afraid not!

Addie My God—what a mess!

Judy (*crossing* R, *her eye on the door, the syringe still poised in her hand*) As you say—a mess! So you're ruined anyway. I shall just have to settle for that.

Justin Hang on a minute—you needn't think you're getting off Scot-free. I heard you confess to murdering Millie—that's when I called the police.

Judy The police...

Justin They're coming now—I've left the stage door open for them.

Judy (*with cold resolution*) The police—no, it's not in the plan. I'm not going to prison. My whole life has been a prison. I'm not going... (*She pumps her arm, her fist clenched*)

Police sirens sound

Justin (*crossing to her*) Give me that syringe.

Judy No—no—no! (*She stabs herself with the syringe, murmuring*) Too late! Going out on a pink cloud... (*Her voice trails away as she falls to her knees and slowly collapses*)

Justin Stupid fool! (*He drops to his knees beside her*)

Addie Will she be all right?

Justin I doubt it.

Judy trembles, then relaxes with a deep sigh

Addie She isn't dead, Justin—she isn't...

Justin I can't feel a pulse...

Addie Oh, God!

Ed and Pearl burst in

Ed The police are outside—what's happened?

Pearl We were just leaving when we saw the police car pull up.

Addie Oh my God—Ed... (*She struggles to rise and throws herself into his arms, crying*) It's awful—the poor girl...

Pearl Judy—you mean...

Addie Yes, Judy.

Justin (*turning to them*) She's dead.

Pearl Dead?

Ed But how?

Addie She's killed herself—oh, Eddie, she's killed herself and she was my daughter!

Ed Your daughter?

Pearl Judy was your daughter!

Addie She killed Millie. She was going to kill me but Justin came in. Oh, it's all my fault.

Ed Darling, she isn't your daughter.

Addie She is, she is. I told you about it, didn't I? Years ago when we were together. You agreed with me it was better to keep quiet—the publicity—and her age, everyone would have worked out how old I was!

Ed Yes, you told me about it—but what I didn't tell you was that I found her, your daughter. I wanted to look after her for you, give her money.

Addie You found her?

Ed No, I didn't actually find her. I looked for her. When I found her she was already dead. She died in a squat in Brixton of a drug overdose when she was sixteen.

Addie But this girl—this girl—who is she?

Ed Who knows?

They all stare at Judy as——

—*the* CURTAIN *falls*

FURNITURE AND PROPERTY LIST

Further dressing may be added at the director's discretion

ACT I

SCENE 1

On stage: Intercom by door
Rack of clothes
Screen
2 dressing-tables with mirrors. *On table* R: make-up items, tissues, etc.
   In drawer of table R: half full bottle of brandy. *On table* L: make-up
   items, hair brush, grubby glasses, make-up towel, etc.
2 chairs
Couch
Addie's dressing-gown

Off stage: Handbag containing key to dressing-table drawer (**Addie**)
Large bouquet (**Pearl**)
Flowers in vase (**Millie**)
2 mugs of tea and bowl of sugar on tray (**Judy**)

Personal: **Addie:** jewellery
Justin: wrist-watch (worn throughout)

SCENE 2

On stage: As before

Set: Evening dress behind screen
Gun in drawer of table R
Brandy on table R
Script on table L
Millie's handbag

ACT II

SCENE 1

On stage: As before

Set: Small stepladder
                  Intercom speaker
                  Large boxes
                  Clothes
                  Clothes rail
                  Shoes

Off stage: 2 cups of tea and bowl of sugar on tray (**Judy**)

SCENE 2

On stage: As before

Set: Clothes rail and most of clothes behind screen
                  Evening dress
                  Tissue paper, string, large pair of scissors
                  Old photographs in drawer of table R
                  Large syringe on dressing-table R

Off stage: Tray with coffee in percolator, two mugs and bowl of sugar (**Judy**)

LIGHTING PLOT

Property fittings required: nil
1 interior. The same throughout

ACT I, SCENE 1

To open: Darkness

Cue 1   **Justin** switches light on   (Page 1)
             Snap on overall lighting

ACT I, SCENE 2

To open: Darkness

Cue 2   **Justin** switches light on   (Page 17)
             Snap on overall lighting

ACT II, SCENE 1

To open: Overall general lighting

No cues

ACT II, SCENE 2

To open: Overall general lighting

No cues

EFFECTS PLOT

ACT I

Cue 1   **Justin**: "...you've had more experience."   (Page 17)
           Sound of applause off

Cue 2   **Ed**: "Solemn promise! Scout's honour!"   (Page 21)
           Softly ring front of house bell off

Cue 3   **Millie**: "I'll make the most of my death scene."   (Page 23)
           Music off

Cue 4   **Addie**: "Of course I am."   (Page 24)
           Gun shot off

Cue 5   **Ed**: "Alive—presumably."   (Page 25)
           Screaming and pandemonium off

ACT II

Cue 6   **Judy** pumps her arm, fist clenched   (Page 47)
           Sound of police sirens off

Lightning Source UK Ltd.
Milton Keynes UK
UKOW06f0659041217
313838UK00004B/18/P